INTRODUCTIO

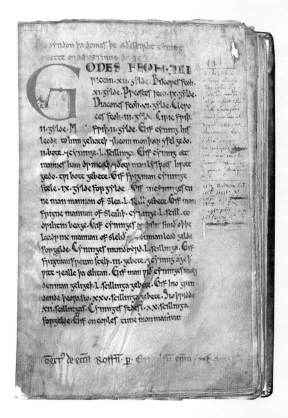

Above: The start of King Ethelbert's law codes. The capital letter 'G' begins the phrase, 'God's property ...' (folio 1r).

In 1122, nearly a century before Magna Carta (1215), a monk in Rochester Cathedral Priory carefully copied out the laws issued by Ethelbert[2], the first Christian King of Kent (r.c.560–616). Ethelbert's law code was the first codified statement of English law written in English. Today, still kept by Rochester Cathedral, this monk's manuscript is the earliest known copy of Ethelbert's Anglo-Saxon law code. It survives within *Textus Roffensis* – the 'Book of Rochester'.

Textus Roffensis is about the size of a hardback novel and is made up of two parts, mostly written by the same monk who copied Ethelbert's law code, and features both Old English – the language of the Anglo-Saxons – and Latin. The first part of *Textus Roffensis* also includes the laws of other Anglo-Saxon kings, and is the most comprehensive collection of ancient English laws surviving today. The second part is a compilation of the oldest cartulary, or register of lands and properties, belonging to Rochester Cathedral Priory.

Following the Norman Conquest, at a time of great change, the monks of Rochester felt their independence and financial security were under threat. To defend themselves and secure their future they compiled *Textus Roffensis*. The book underlined the rich heritage of Rochester Cathedral Priory, its role in establishing Christianity in England, and provided the monks with an effective legal document with which to reinforce their claims to privileges and possessions.

Textus Roffensis reveals the traditions of early medieval monastic life and literacy, and is crucial to our understanding of the development of English law and language. History may have shone a brighter light on Magna Carta, but it has been said there are few books of such importance for understanding the development of English civilisation as *Textus Roffensis*.[3]

Opposite: The impressive West Front of Rochester Cathedral today.

LIFE IN MEDIEVAL ENGLAND

ife was very different in the 12th century when *Textus Roffensis* was written. Christianity formed the bedrock of society and the medieval church was a pillar of political and economic power. Religious observance and the Christian calendar ordered the daily routine, determining not only when Easter and Christmas were, but also when ploughing and shearing were done.

The rhythm and cycle of agriculture were central to medieval life. Bread was the mainstay of the medieval diet and ale (sweeter and thicker than it is today), rather than water, was the main beverage.

War, violence, accident and disease were constant threats, and a poor harvest and famine meant illness and death; most people died in their thirties or forties. However, the wholesome diet of our medieval ancestors meant that they grew about as tall as us with healthy bones and teeth.

In 1086, almost 40 years before the writing of *Textus Roffensis*, Domesday Book recorded the population of England at around 1.5 million: towns and communities were small and the countryside was sparsely populated. Most buildings were modest, made from wood, thatch and plaster. Only large churches, cathedrals and castles were made of stone.

The words and pictures in manuscripts like *Textus Roffensis* show a world in many ways alien to our own. Yet they also depict people like us; people with the same physical attributes, emotions, concerns with justice, and the same worries and humour that we too experience.

Above: A list of seven archangels included in the second part of Textus Roffensis *(folio 116v).*

THE FOUNDATION OF ROCHESTER CATHEDRAL PRIORY AND GROWTH OF ITS BOOK COLLECTION

ochester Cathedral was founded in 604 following the conversion of King Ethelbert of Kent to Christianity. It was a small, poor foundation that did not thrive as a centre of learning. Following the Norman Conquest (1066), Rochester was re-founded as a Benedictine cathedral priory. As a Benedictine house, reading featured daily in the life of the cathedral. The monks were expected to spend three or four hours reading at fixed times throughout the day. Subsequently, Rochester witnessed a remarkable growth in book production.

A COMMUNITY PROJECT

Below: The current binding on Textus Roffensis.

A community of highly skilled monks would have worked as a team to prepare parchment, mix inks, sharpen quills, write and bind books. In an age before the printing press, the only means to reproduce a document was to painstakingly copy it out by hand. Copying manuscripts required acute skills and only after thousands of hours of practice could medieval scribes attain near perfect coordination so that every stroke of each letter could be made instinctively, without thought. Twelve monks worked in the scriptorium at Rochester, which was built on the south side of the cathedral for maximum warmth and light.

To produce their books the monks in Rochester borrowed exemplars, or samples, from other cathedrals – frequently Christ Church, Canterbury – from which to make copies. These books were often about the history of the Christian church and its founders, but the Rochester scribes also wrote their own books about the history of their cathedral, and kept careful records of its rights and possessions.

TEXTUS ROFFENSIS:
A BOOK OF TWO PARTS

 oday we think of *Textus Roffensis* as a finished product, a single bound book. However, it was not planned and constructed that way. Its two distinct parts were written separately, and each has its own title. The first part was completed in 1122 and entitled *Incipiunt quedam instituta de legibus regum anglorum.*[4] The second part was written *c.*1125 and its title was *Incipiunt privilegia aecclesie sancti andreae hrofensis concessa a tempore ethilberhti regis, qui fide christiana a beato augustino suscepta, eandem ecclesiam construe fecit.*[5]

At the end of the second part is a list of books belonging to the Cathedral Priory; this includes the title of the first part, suggesting that it was, at one time, a separate book.

The second part does not seem to have been bound up as a book to begin with, but simply kept as a loose collection of manuscripts.

Below left: This is an agreement between Bishop Gundulf and Edmund of London concerning property. Much of the original text appears to have been erased and written over (folio 210v).

Below right: 'Dom be haten isene an waetre'. This code concerns managing trials by ordeal using hot iron and water (folios 32r, 32v).

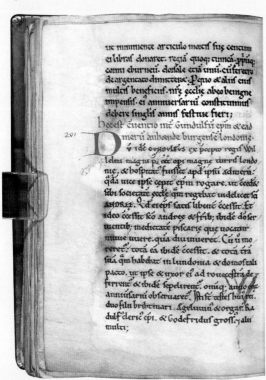

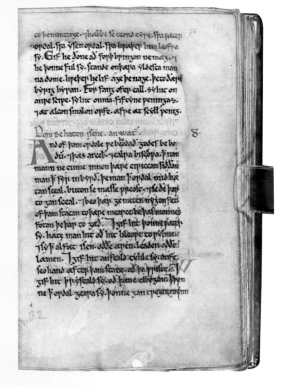

FORGERY?

One intriguing theory to explain why the contents of the book were bound together and called a 'textus' is that the monks of Rochester were attempting to hide evidence of forged manuscripts.

By the 13th century some say the monks at Rochester had become experts in forging documents concerning the Cathedral Priory's heritage, property possessions, and privileges. In an attempt to conceal documents that might prove embarrassing to the monks if they fell into the wrong hands, it has been suggested that the forged manuscripts were interleaved with the genuine, original manuscripts in the second part of the book. These were then bound beneath the first part and the leaves trimmed as necessary to ensure they would fit under the boards, taken from a precious gospel book that few people would want to read.[6]

WHY WERE THE TWO PARTS BOUND TOGETHER?

By the end of the 13th century both parts were bound as a single book, and by the early 14th century it was inscribed with the words *Textus de ecclesia Roffensi per Enulfum episcopum* ('Special book of the church of Rochester by, or from, Bishop Ernulf').

The term 'textus' was usually reserved for gospel, or particularly precious books that were kept in the church, so by calling the book a 'textus' the monks were marking it out as being of exceptional importance.

We may never know for sure why the two different parts were eventually bound together by the monks, but binding was expensive so the content was clearly very valuable to the Cathedral Priory of Rochester.

5

WHO WROTE THE BOOK?

Although the two parts of *Textus Roffensis* were written a few years apart, they look to have been written by the same hand. We may never know the identity of the scribe, but it has been suggested that it was either Rochester's Precentor – a monk called Hunfid – or Ordwine, the Prior of Rochester. Whoever he was, he was skilled in writing both Latin and Old English.

THE SCRIPT

Each monastery developed its own writing style. Rochester's scriptorium produced a distinctive 'prickly' script style, and an emphasis on plain books. The scribes focused on reproducing texts accurately rather than on decoration and illumination.

INK AND ILLUMINATION

Iron gall ink was commonly used in the scriptorium. It was made from readily available ingredients, did not clog up the writing tool, and was indelible and fade resistant. These characteristics meant that it remained popular, particularly for use on official documents, until well into the

Below: 'The Unknown Scribe'. This evocative artwork, created by Carol Norton and Madeline Hazelden, can be found at Rochester Cathedral.

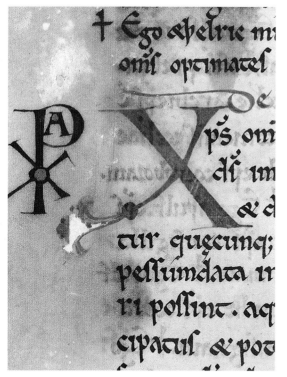

20th century. A key ingredient of the ink was oak galls – marble-sized swellings produced by an oak tree after an insect such as a wasp has laid its eggs in the tree's bark.

Ink was known as encaustum, from the Latin *caustere* ('to bite') because when used on parchment it literally ate into the parchment's surface. In some cases, over time, the acid content of the ink has caused damage to manuscripts.

A process of mixing, grinding and heating ingredients from a wide variety of minerals, plants and animals could produce a range of colours for the illuminator to use.

There is a single illumination in *Textus Roffensis*. At the start of the second part of the book there is a striking, decorated capital 'R'. A saint or Christ-like figure, and some dragons or serpents, picked out in green, yellow, red and a purple-blue colour, form the letter 'R'. The figure has his right hand raised with the first two fingers and thumb extended and the third and fourth fingers closed over, making the sign of Christian benediction. He may also have the marks of stigmata on his feet. He stands upright upon a dragon or serpent-like creature, symbolising, perhaps, the vanquishing of Satan. Next to him is a larger, more animated dragon, or serpent. A similar creature sprouting acanthus leaves is disappearing into, or coming out of, its mouth.

THE PAGES

The pages (known as leaves, or folios) of both parts of *Textus Roffensis* are made of high-quality vellum, a form of parchment made from calfskin. Before the scribe could set to work, the parchment had to be prepared. After the animal had been slaughtered and flayed, its hair, fat and flesh were removed. This was a smelly, messy process, which involved soaking hides in various mixtures, including lime, animal faeces and eggs.

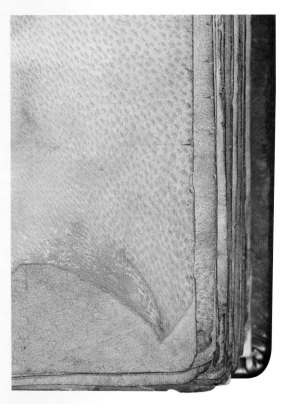

The hide was rinsed to remove any acid, before being stretched out on a frame so it could be scraped and shaved. It would be left to dry and then further shaved and scraped, and then trimmed.

The surface of the folios of the first part of the book has been scraped and sanded to a fine, velvety finish; something that is difficult to achieve even with a modern electric sander! On the leaves of the second part, much of the animal's hair follicle pattern is still intact.

Above: The hair follicles on the calfskin can clearly be seen (folio 56r).

Finally, holes would be pricked in the vellum and lines, for the scribe to follow, were scored between them with a hard point – the back of a knife, for example.

Above: Grazing rights enabling the monks to fatten up livestock such as pigs were a vital part of the Cathedral Priory's livelihood. Documents granting rights are an important feature of the second part of Textus Roffensis © *The British Library Board (Royal 2 B. VII, f.81v).*

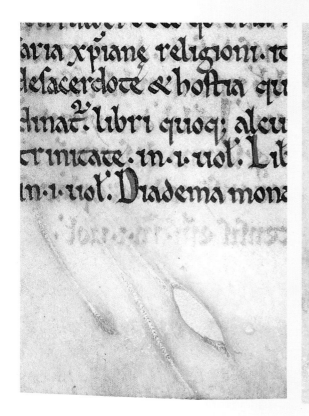

aria xpiane religioni. te
lesacerdote & hostia qu
dmae. libri quoq; alcu
ct unitate. in. v. uol. Lit
in. 1. uol. Diadema monr

Above left: A small, oval-shaped hole in the vellum might be the result of an injury to the animal when it was alive, an insect bite, or a small tear made during the scraping and stretching of the vellum. This type of parchment was expensive so the scribe has written around the hole (folio 217r).

Above right: Water damage to Textus Roffensis (folio 206v).

Right: The pricking and scoring by a monk almost 1,000 years ago can still be seen. To speed up the process, many leaves of vellum were often pricked at the same time and then opened up so that the lines could be scored between them (folio 5r).

Vellum is a durable writing material but sensitive to changes in humidity levels. Fluctuations in humidity can cause parchment to 'cockle', or pucker, and, occasionally, shadows of the ribs of an animal long since dead may be seen on a page.

BINDING

Nothing certain is known about the early bindings of *Textus Roffensis*. Its medieval binding would have involved sewing together the loose leaves to form a text block, which would have been laced onto wooden boards through channels that had been carved and burnt into them. Medieval books were sometimes further enclosed in a loose leather or textile cover, known as a chemise, which folded over the fore-edge of the book. Relatively few examples of these have survived.

The current binding of *Textus Roffensis* is tanned brown calfskin.

THE FIRST PART:
THE LAW BOOK

n compiling the first part of *Textus Roffensis*, the scribe has drawn together a vast range of law codes from the kings of Kent and Wessex in order to emphasise the continued authority and legitimacy of Anglo-Saxon law in an England dominated by Norman legal practices.

ETHELBERT'S LAW CODE

When King Ethelbert converted to Christianity he moved away from the Anglo-Saxon tradition of passing on customs and laws by word of mouth, and embraced the Christian tradition of writing laws down rather than trusting them to memory. In doing this he set a precedent that later kings of the Anglo-Saxon period followed.

The language and details of Ethelbert's laws may seem strange today but they concern issues which are still relevant: the role of government, the security of property, sexual aggression and women's rights, and compensation for death or injury.

These law codes show that English society was beginning to move away from retributive justice (for example, 'an eye for an eye') towards a codified system of law in which a dispute was settled once and for all with a payment of money.

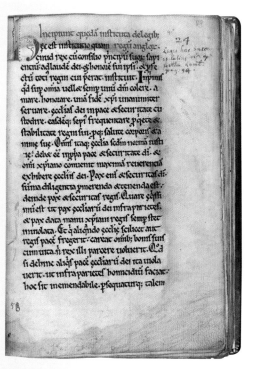

Above: It is likely that folio 58 (shown here) was originally the first page of what is now Textus Roffensis. At some date unknown the folios were reshuffled and bound in the order we find them today.

Right: A seated scribe, holding quill and pen knife, with an ink horn and exemplars weighted down upon a stand. The scriptorium at Rochester might have resembled the modest one pictured here, as it was a relatively poor foundation © The British Library Board (Royal 14 E. III, f.6v).

In 1922 Frederick Attenborough – father of actor and director Sir Richard Attenborough and broadcaster and naturalist Sir David Attenborough – published The Laws of the Earliest English Kings. *His book featured a number of the law codes copied into* Textus Roffensis *and became the standard work on the subject for many decades.*

Below left: The importance of Rochester Bridge is indicated by this manuscript which concerns responsibility for its maintenance and repair. This leaf is a replacement and there is evidence of amendments to the text, suggesting that it may have been tampered with (folio 166v).

Below right: Some of Ethelbert's law codes copied in Old English into Textus Roffensis *(folios 1v, 2r).*

In King Ethelbert's code, for example, if an ear was struck off, 12 shillings in compensation was to be paid; if an eye was put out, compensation was 50 shillings; for the loss of the four front teeth, 6 shillings for each; if someone struck another on the nose with a fist, 3 shillings compensation was due; if a person broke into a commoner's home he was to compensate with 6 shillings; accomplices who entered after the person who broke in must pay 3 shillings and thereafter one shilling according to the order in which they broke in.

The few rights that women had were understood in terms of their value to the males in their family. For example: a widow could retain her husband's goods, even if she remarried, but only if she had borne him children; if someone took a girl by force, the code states, 50 shillings compensation was due to her protector.

An important feature of these law codes was that they were written in English rather than Latin. Old English was the language of the Anglo-Saxons and Ethelbert's law code is the earliest text to resemble the language we use today.

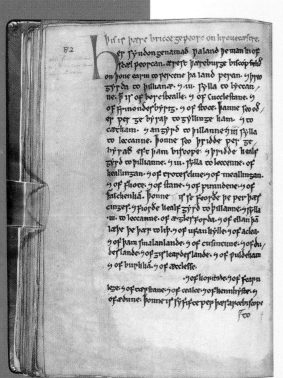

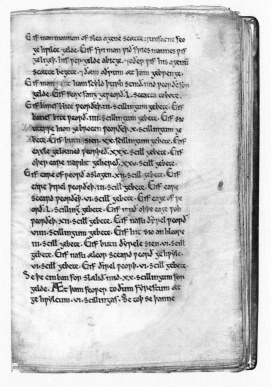

THE CORONATION CHARTER OF HENRY I

Included in the first part of *Textus Roffensis* is a copy of the coronation charter of Henry I from *c*.1100. Copied by the Rochester scribe in its original Latin, this is the oldest existing copy of Henry's charter. Henry made it clear to the barons that he was moving away from 'all the bad customs by which the realm of England was unjustly oppressed'.

Henry's charter explains the responsibilities and limits of the king towards the church and his noblemen. It has been said that Henry's charter influenced the wording of Magna Carta and even the American Declaration of Independence (1776).[7]

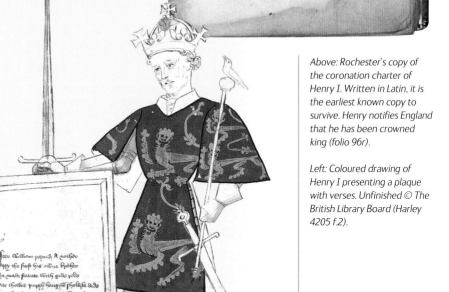

Above: Rochester's copy of the coronation charter of Henry I. Written in Latin, it is the earliest known copy to survive. Henry notifies England that he has been crowned king (folio 96r).

Left: Coloured drawing of Henry I presenting a plaque with verses. Unfinished © The British Library Board (Harley 4205 f.2).

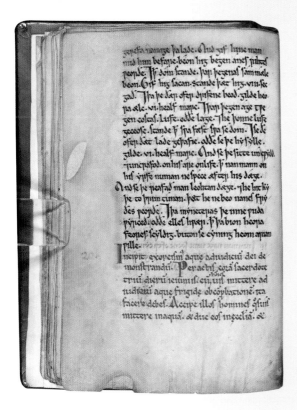

Above left: Three forms of 'exorcism', or ordeal, are laid out over the next nine folios – one for water, one for iron and one for bread. It starts: 'Here begins the exorcism of water to demonstrate God's judgment' (folios 49v and 50r).

Above right: Charm for recovering stolen livestock (folio 95r).

MAGIC, CHARMS AND ORDEALS

Lists of kings, emperors, popes, bishops and even archangels are featured in *Textus Roffensis*, alongside accounts of the ceremonial ordeals to test innocence by red-hot irons and boiling water, magical charms to find stolen animals, and an excommunication curse.

Anglo-Saxon charms were used widely: to ward off evil, heal the sick and to recover lost animals, for instance. The charm shown here is written in Old English and Latin and mixes magic with Christian references. It begins: 'If it is a horse [that is stolen], sing [the charm] upon its ... bridle.'

THE SECOND PART: THE CARTULARY OF ROCHESTER CATHEDRAL PRIORY

 ost of the second part of *Textus Roffensis* is a cartulary: a compilation of charters in book form. Written in Latin, the charters record legal grants of land, property and rights. Each property or place is highlighted on the page with a coloured capital letter to make it quick to locate a particular document.

King William II (r.1087–1100) appears to have offered land in Buckinghamshire to Rochester Cathedral Priory, on the condition that Bishop Gundulf built a stone castle at Rochester for the king. The monks seem to have agreed to this, but made it clear that they would not be responsible for the castle's future upkeep. The document points out that as long as the castle exists, the lands in Buckinghamshire will belong to the monks of Rochester.

Above: This early charter, witnessed by King Eardwulf of Kent and the Archbishop of Canterbury in 762, grants to Rochester Cathedral Priory the rights of local pasture to 12 herds of pigs. Anyone who infringed this right would be condemned to eternal damnation (folio 123r).

The last section of *Textus Roffensis* is made up of miscellaneous documents, in both Old English and Latin, including lists of donors, grants, offices and payments, a list of knights, and a catalogue of the books held by Rochester Cathedral Priory. These manuscripts were written to demonstrate Rochester Cathedral's historical, religious and legal legitimacy.

Right: Listed later in the book by a different scribe is a copy of a 'papal bull' granting certain rights and privileges to the monastery at Rochester in the name of Pope Eugene III (1145–53). The mysterious-looking circular image represents the Pope's seal. The term 'bull' comes from the word bulla, Latin for 'seal' (folios 207v and 208r).

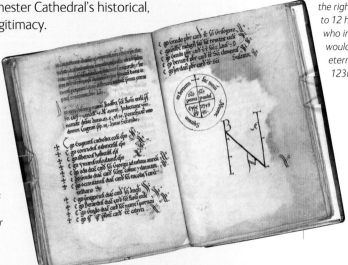

'LOST' AND 'FOUND'

LIBRARY LEGACY

Today, books bearing the inscription of Rochester Cathedral Priory – liber de claustro Roffensi – can be found in libraries around the world.

ccasional additions were made to the contents of *Textus Roffensis* up until the early 14th century. At this point the book seems to have disappeared.

With the dissolution of the monasteries in 1540, Rochester's book collection was dispersed. Almost 100 books were taken into the Royal Collection, now at the British Library. However, for some reason *Textus Roffensis* remained in Rochester.

Hidden, lost, or simply forgotten about, it was not until 1573 that William Lambarde, a historian who could read Old English, 're-discovered' *Textus Roffensis*. Over the following 400 years and more, *Textus Roffensis* was the subject of research and enquiry by many scholars and historians. In 1630, one Dr Leonard took the book for his own purposes, and only after a lengthy legal battle was it returned in 1633 to Rochester Cathedral. It survived the English Civil War, and in 1712 Elizabeth Elstob had the second part transcribed in three months by a child prodigy, James Smith. Elizabeth Elstob herself is said to have written the list of 'Saxon characters' shown here and initialled 'E.E.'

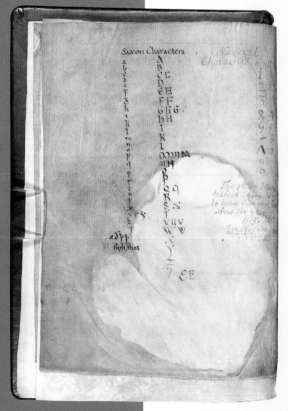

Left: A list of Saxon characters added to Textus Roffensis *in the early 18th century, probably by Elizabeth Elstob. Traces of human activity over successive centuries are suggested by later annotations (folio iiiv).*

Dr John Harris, a Canon of Rochester, appears to have had *Textus Roffensis* in his possession for a considerable time while he was writing his *History of Kent* (1719). It was probably during this time that the book suffered the water damage still visible today. Accounts suggest that *Textus Roffensis*, travelling by boat between Rochester and London, was dropped into either the River Thames or the Medway. Little is known about what actually happened, but the pattern of the staining suggests that the book's straps and brass clasps did their job in holding it tightly closed and limiting the amount of water able to get between the leaves. Perhaps because of the damage sustained as a result of this incident, *Textus Roffensis* was rebound in 1718.

Records suggest it may have been rebound at least once since then, and show that in 1937 *Textus Roffensis* was deposited with the British Museum for conservation treatment, which included a new binding. Nonetheless, surprisingly little is known about the conservation work to *Textus Roffensis*, even during recent years. Sadly, over the years, most medieval bindings on books have been replaced for conservation reasons or simply because of changes in taste and fashion.[8]

Above: The box that until recently housed Textus Roffensis *and its companion, the early 13th-century* Custumale Roffense.

NOTES

1   Old English Riddle 26 from the 'Exeter Book' in Wilcox, Jonathan (ed.), *Scraped, Stroked and Bound: Materially Engaged Readings of Medieval Manuscripts* (Turnhout, Belgium: Brepols, 2013), pp. viii–ix

2   'Æthelbehrt' is often how the Kentish king's name appears in print, but in order to be consistent with the style of Rochester Cathedral's interpretive text, 'Ethelbert' is the spelling used in this guide

3   Michael Wood suggests that *Textus Roffensis* may be one of the most important manuscripts in the history of English civilisation in *The Textus Roffensis: a Hidden Treasure*, an interpretation film (Rochester Cathedral, 2013)

4   Translation: 'Some enactments from the laws of the kings of the English'

5   Translation: 'Privileges granted to the church of St Andrew of Rochester, from the time of King Æthelberht who, converted to Christianity by St Augustine, caused the church to be built'

6   Colin Flight, 'The Making of the *Textus Roffensis*', www.kentarchaeology.ac/digiarchive/colinflight/bmr-textus.pdf, p. 101, as of 7 January 2014

7   Patrick Wormald, *The First Code of English Law* (Canterbury, The Canterbury Commemoration Society, 2005), unnumbered centre pages

8   Dean and Chapter of Rochester Cathedral Minute Books 1575–1968; 1937:DRC/AC 29 (23.02.37 and 16.03.37); Medway Archives and Local Studies Centre

Back Cover: Detail from the fresco in the North Transept of Rochester Cathedral, showing the baptism of King Ethelbert (painted by Sergey Fyodorov).

CONCLUSION

extus Roffensis is a remarkable book. Today, when we touch Textus Roffensis, we are touching the past, but not just a single moment in history. Over many years, layers of human memories and associations with people, places, events and animals have been laid down in this single book.

It is neither large nor ornate, yet it contains an incomparable collection of laws from the Anglo-Saxon period, it is an important record of the development of the English language, and is key to the early history of Rochester Cathedral. Together, the two parts of Textus Roffensis represent an immensely valuable source of knowledge and understanding of the Anglo-Saxon and Anglo-Norman periods.

It seems highly likely that the scribe's motivation for writing the book was the preservation of the Anglo-Saxon heritage of Rochester Cathedral Priory, and its future in Norman England during a time of great social, political and religious uncertainty. It is perhaps testament to the success of Textus Roffensis in achieving this that Rochester Cathedral has survived and thrived into the 21st century.

You can now see the whole book in amazing detail online:
http://luna.manchester.ac.uk/luna/servlet/s/0q5kpi

ACKNOWLEDGEMENTS

The author would like to thank Gwen Riley Jones and Carol Burrows, at the Centre for Heritage Imaging and Collections Care, University of Manchester (CHICC), Lizzie Bradshaw, Helen Bradshaw, Suzy Micklewright, Dr Chris Monk (www. anglosaxonmonk.com) and Gilly Wilford for their invaluable help in producing this guide. Also for the help and expert guidance of Abbie Wood and Susan Swalwell at Pitkin Publishing. And last but by no means least, Anna O'Neill who makes everything possible. Any and all errors are my own.

Text written by Armand De Filippo. The author has asserted his moral rights.

Edited by Abbie Wood.
Designed by Jemma Cox.

All images of pages of Textus Roffensis were digitised by the Centre for Heritage Imaging and Collections Care, John Rylands Library, University of Manchester, and reproduced courtesy of Rochester Cathedral. All other images are reproduced by the kind permission of the following: Lizzie Bradshaw: inside front cover, p.6; Centre for Heritage Imaging and Collections Care,

John Rylands Library, University of Manchester: pp.5, 16; British Library: pp.8b, 10b, 12b; David Robinson/Rochester Cathedral: back cover.

Every effort has been made to contact copyright holders; the publisher will be pleased to rectify any omissions in future editions.

Publication in this form © Pitkin Publishing 2015.
No part of this publication may be reproduced, stored in a retrieval system or transmitted in any form or by any means without the permission of Pitkin Publishing and the copyright holders.

ISBN 978-1-84165-618-2   1/15

Pitkin Publishing. The History Press, The Mill, Brimscombe Port, Stroud, Gloucestershire GL5 2QG.

Enquiries and sales: 01453 883300
Email: sales@thehistorypress.co.uk
www.thehistorypress.co.uk

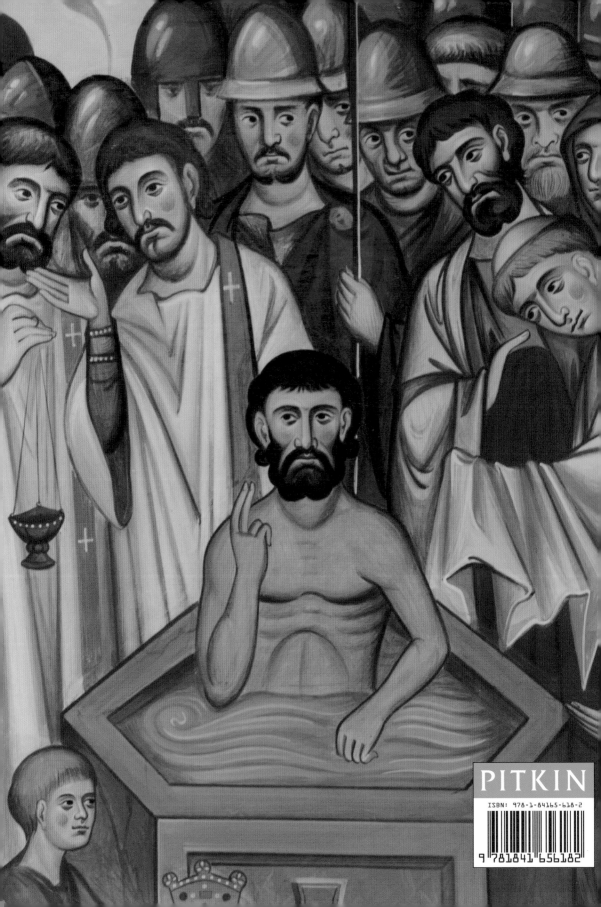

PITKIN

ISBN: 978-1-84165-618-2